Unapologetically Myself

e.a.c.

Thankful

For my brothers, everything I do is for you. For my parents, for my friends who have stuck by my side, and those friends who have left, for everyone who has come in and out of my life, for everyone who chooses to stay. Thank you for the endless lessons you have taught me, for your guidance, for your love. For making me who I am, for showing me who I am not. I truly do not know where I would be without each and every person who has deeply affected my perspective and changed my life. For better or for worse, I dedicate it all to you.

A Letter to the Reader-

I have been a lot of things in my life, some pure and some tortured. I have felt a lot of emotions in my life, some dreadful and some breathtaking. Although I truly am at peace with myself now, not everything is perfect. There are no *truly* happy endings, and some days I still struggle even more than I did way back when. The two halves of this book do not represent that everything will clear up, and that you will one day look back on your life with ease and forget what pain feels like. But the two halves of this book really do show a turning point in my life, and I want you all to experience it without any sugarcoating. I want you to learn and grow with me, I want you to feel pain and rejoice with me. I wish you the best with your story, and I am overjoyed to show mine to you, raw and unfiltered.

"Because of you"

"Because of You"

Because of You

Flashbacks

I get flashbacks

Skin crawling, Heart racing

Mind panicking, Body quivering

All cause my first

Was not pure or loving

Or even my choice

Forever tainted, this act

Beautiful, intimate

No more

Because of you

I have let go as much as

I possibly can

However,

Small parts of me

Will always remember

How wrong it all was

And how ugly

I still feel

Inside and out

e.a.c.

"Because of You"

My tears will wash off

Tears reaching the floor

Bathroom tile forever stained

Like my underwear

e.a.c.

"Because of You"

Never the Same

My hands tremulous

My heart clobbering

My mind

      Flying

            Rushing

                Hastening

All because

I thought I saw him

Nothing extraordinary

This panic and terror have

Just become me

e.a.c.

Your Fault

He took her inside

Coerced her with conversation

One thing

Led to another

She shook her head

And said no

No

No

But he was not asking for permission

She went home

Never telling anyone

Never saying a word

Maybe she was cowardly

For being silenced

But he was the real coward

For destroying

What was not his

e.a.c.

"Because of You"

Forever

Did you know that after kissing someone

Their bacteria creates

Microbiomes in your mouth

That last as long as you do

Maybe that is why despite

The number of showers I take or the

Days that go by, I will still

Feel him

Forcing himself on me

e.a.c.

My Heart, a Playground

He only wants to be around me when he can

Touch me, grab me

All I am to him is a physical fantasy

He is never looking in my eyes, only at my body

When he speaks to me intimately

It is all fun and games to him

He uses my weaknesses as manipulation

And plays on my insecurities like a swing set

As if I am here for his pleasure only

Nothing more, everything less

So why did I stay with him

Eating up his lies

Ignoring my intended purpose

Because after hearing this is all I am worth

Time and time again

I eventually began to believe it

e.a.c.

"Because of You"

Empty

Looking in his eyes

I will never understand

The lack of remorse

e.a.c.

"Because of You"

Amnesia

I wish I could forget

The way he grabbed me

I wish I could forget

The roughness of his hands

Or how vulgar he was with me

But I could never get rid of

These memories

These horror stories

But I am sure he has forgotten with ease

e.a.c.

Side Effects of Tragedy

First it starts with a frown

Then leads to tears

Flowing down

Everyone has a way to cope

But eventually some lose all hope

This poor girl does not know what to do

Therapy, medicine, psychiatrists too

But nothing seems to get her through

Cuts on her wrists and all up her thigh

Drinking occasionally

Smoking every day to get by

Unconventional, unhealthy, yes

But that is what grief does to us

I guess

e.a.c.

"Because of You"

Superficial

Every boy looks after me with lust

Usually I am perfectly content

With the above

Lately I long for love

I do not always want to touch

Sometimes that is too much

I do not always desire sex

I want something far more complex

I am tired of these up and down stares

I need something that can honestly compare

Usually I am perfectly content

With these thoughts

Lately I am utterly distraught

e.a.c.

"Because of You"

Colder

She put flowers in her hair

She wore them everywhere

She slept in daisies

Awoke with lilies

And wore roses for special

Occasions

But the weather grew colder

And the flowers stopped growing

The girl was bewildered

She only knew of Spring's

Beginning

But soon she'd have to fight Winter's

End

e.a.c.

Perspective

She was like a glass

Optimists saw her as

Halfway full

Pessimist claimed she was

Half empty

Realists said she was

Simply half

But she knew herself as

Completely absent

Utterly barren

Nothing could possibly

Fill her up

e.a.c.

Scapegoat

A fire burned inside of him

It provided him warmth

It made him feel at ease

But somedays

The fire overwhelmed him

Consumed him

Devoured everything that he

Previously understood

Of himself

It made him dangerous

It made others afraid

This wasn't really him

It was the fire inside

But he was always blamed

e.a.c.

Venomous

They tell me to write what I know

And as these pages

Fill with poison, pain, and agony

I realize that is all that is inside of me

e.a.c.

"Because of You"

Burden

Whenever I call my friends

They answer in a hurry

All with the same first response

'Is everything okay'

I can practically see the

Worry on their faces

I can hear them

Holding their breathe tensely

I have become a ticking time bomb and

Everyone in my life is bracing for

My explosion

When did I become that girl,

Well, less of a girl and more of

A worry, a threat

I hope when I detonate

I only leave a path of self-destruction

But even a simple phone call reminds me

Of the innocent casualties

I may cause

e.a.c.

"Because of You"

Public Places

When they stare at him

I want us to disappear

Shield us from their eyes

e.a.c.

The Familiar Stranger

Some days

When I allow myself to think too much

Or when I get too much fresh air

When I spend too much time alone

Or when my thoughts go elsewhere

Something unsettling grows inside me

It always resides deep in my bones

It makes my stomach churn

It makes my heart plea

But most of all

It makes me

Restless

Wild

Unhappy

e.a.c.

"Because of You"

Prisoner

I always laugh and flip my hair

Maybe even roll my eyes and say I don't care

Wow girl, you are so strong and kind

You seem so free thinking and unconfined

But then I go home and lay in bed

Cry violently, even wish that I was dead

Why am I like this

Why can my thoughts not dismiss

I wish on the inside I was what they saw

But I'm not and I can't be

It's unwritten law

e.a.c.

"Because of You"

Our Lives

At a glance

He just looks gloomy

She just looks skinny

She just seems angry

He just seems lonely

At a glance

You could never tell

They are each going

Through a hell

Clinging onto life

While each one of us

Just survives

e.a.c.

Just Look on the Bright Side

If they only knew how much I would give

So that I did not feel this way

I would give it all, I would give my life

Oh, how I've tried

e.a.c.

Alice Cannot Withstand

Meditation

Or

Medication

It does not make a difference

On days like today

My depression and anxiety will not listen

During therapy, writing their own rules

And if I do not follow along

Even the birds will sing sad songs

Everything so dreary and bleak

For me, a girl who is so weak

The thought of being in control

Causes my anxiety and depression to

Shove me down a rabbit hole

e.a.c.

Sirens

Way beyond the shore

Deep in the ocean

Lives a girl, forevermore

Way past the current

Down below the surface

She stays subservient

She listens to the wave

Obeys the tide always

Waiting to save

Humans they would drown

And the girls' job was to rescue

Before they could even frown

Just once, she thought

I can save a human for me

And at last I will have some company

But that is not what the tide taught

So there she lays

Way beyond the shore

For the rest of her days

All alone, unknown, never shown

e.a.c.

"Because of You"

Get Away While You Can

'My mind is a mess' I would always say

'No it's not, let us see' they would always insist

Eventually I would shrug my shoulders

And let them in

They would take one look

And run far away

'I told you it was bad' I would call

'We've seen bad, and this is much worse' they would yell

While they are running I bet they

Never think what it's like to be me

Trapped in this mess for eternity

e.a.c.

"Because of You"

Reality

I wish things were different

I wish I wasn't me

I wish I was significant

Genies, dandelions,

Shooting stars, too

In the movies there is three wishes

In life there is no guarantees

e.a.c.

"Because of You"

Timing

He kept his bird in a cage

Afraid she would fly away

The bird just needed to

Stretch

And promised to return

Years passed

And he finally let his bird

Stretch her wings

Trusting she would return

But she tasted freedom

And never turned back

Because the time it took for

The man to trust her

Was the same amount of time for

The bird to lose her faith

In the man

e.a.c.

- I want to trust you but I can't, not after all you have done to me, set me free

Insanity

I was hallucinating

Creepy things

Crawly things

It's just my eyes playing tricks on me

That's what they would say

But don't all crazy people start that way

Reality or over active imagination

The lines are blurred

Please tell me I'm not

Absurd

It's absolute mayhem inside my brain

Chaos

Mania

I always knew I was insane

e.a.c.

"Because of You"

Take Shelter

A storm was brewing

Deep inside her

She tried to contain it

But she knew the

Inevitable

Her lightning would strike

And her thunder roar

So she became an outcast

Living in isolation

Because a storm was coming

And she could not stop

The downpour

But maybe she could

Hold out an umbrella

e.a.c.

"Because of You"

My Bed is My Only Companion

They say loneliness is a feeling you get

When you are 'in desperate need of yourself'

Well then what do you call

This feeling of suffocation

Because in everything I do

I am entirely alone

No one behind me or beside me

Thankful when a stranger passing me by

Gives me a smile like a secret

What do you call when no one wants

To spend time with you

Not even yourself

e.a.c.

"Because of You"

Space Girl

A flying saucer dropped me off

Here on Earth

Because I did not look like a creature

From a galaxy far beyond

I appeared to belong with humans

Before dropping me off they failed to realize

On the inside

I was a being from galaxies beyond

Looking like I belong

Does not mean I haven't been an alien all along

e.a.c.

Unwritten

Everyone compliments my writing as

A talent, a blessing, a gift

But often I write what is hurting me

Hoping that letting it go on paper

Will let it seep out of my mind

But the pain is everlasting

And my brokenness is looked at with awe

My most vulnerable moments

Critiqued like a measureable talent

But I am left with curses of a broken mind

e.a.c.

The Same Story

She writes poems to

Feel something at the end of the day

He writes rhymes to

Escape what is outside his door

He writes books to

Distract from what's really out there

She reads novels to

Pretend she's not in reality

In the end

We are all alike

Desperate for something

More or less

Than what we are

e.a.c.

Reminiscing

As I remember

The good old days I begin

To ask what was good

e.a.c.

Keep Your Head Up

There was a boy who

Wanted to reach the peak

Of a mountain

So he treaded onward

Looking up towards his goals

Celebrating his progress

There was a man who

Wanted to reach the peak

Of a mountain

So he treaded onward

Looking down at his feet

Skeptical if he was making

Any progress at all

The boy reached the peak easily

And rejoiced

The man turned back to the summit

And crumbled

e.a.c.

Hallucination

I thought I saw him there

Out in the open air

Then I opened my eyes

And it was all a lie

I thought I saw him next to me

Come here I said with urgency

But then I blinked

And my heart did sink

What appeared to be a

Sweet, treasured dream

Has turned into

An absolute nightmare

e.a.c.

"Because of You"

Niagara Falls

Cascading powerfully

Every drop emphasized

The boy had never seen

Anything like it

There was no comparison

Nothing more

Magic, tragic

Than the waterfall

Streaming down her cheeks

e.a.c.

Destined for Disaster

He was fire

I was water

Our love was

Unattainable

For he could not

Be satiated

And I could not

Glow

e.a.c.

"Because of You"

Surprise

Balloons and confetti

Her surprise party contained

Everyone smiling and cheering

Because it was her birthday

The panic set in

She tried to be happy

Tried to rejoice

But being the center of attention

Was not her first choice

She painted on a smile

But that night she wept

Feeling vulnerable, naked

All eyes on her

Just wasn't her style

e.a.c.

"Because of You"

Undesirable

I have a dilemma, I'm caught in a bind

My hands are tied

I love a boy

Who has left me for her

I have a dilemma, I'm caught in a bind

My hands are tied

I am a mess

And he loves best dressed

I have a dilemma, I'm caught in a bind

My hands are tied

I love a boy

Who doesn't love me

e.a.c.

"Because of You"

Poetic Justice

She stabbed him in the back

He was so hurt,

Alone, Betrayed

He hungered for justice

Desperate for her to feel just as he did

So he stabbed her in the heart

But as he looked into her eyes

He realized with horror

Revenge and justice

Are not the same

e.a.c.

"Because of You"

Reflection and Refraction

Did you know

That people do not have blue eyes

Rather a lack of any color

Blue eyes are just a reflection of

The color they cannot obtain

Maybe that is why I fell in love with

His brown eyes

Full of color

Full of everything I could not be

What I needed most

How could I be so stupid

After all of this time

My eyes are still blue

And his brown

Him so full of what I need

And me, empty

e.a.c.

- I didn't expect my eyes to turn brown but I expected him to fucking try for me

"Because of You"

Fall

He stepped on the beautiful

Autumn leaves

Just as carelessly as he

Stepped on her beautiful

Autumn heart

e.a.c.

"Because of You"

Stonewall

They try and beat me

Defeat me

They want to make me crack

But my titanium skin

Won't let them win

The harder they push

The more they hurt

Little do they know

Even with my skin of titanium

My interior is made of glass

And long ago they shattered me

e.a.c.

"Because of You"

Heroin

When he first ran through my veins

I thought it was exhilarating,

I was invincible, I could feel no pain

I was on top of the world, I trusted him

The high I was left with was insane

Then he began cutting through my veins

I was confused, shocked, how inhumane

Oh but when he left my veins

I was irrational, deranged, filled with strain

I blamed myself, why could he

No longer find comfort within me

What I did not see is that

Impurities like him do not take comfort in love

They take comfort in destroying a girl

They can dispose of

e.a.c.

"Because of You"

The Only Anecdote

In the middle of the night

I will wake up in a panic

And feel like the walls are closing in

I'll jump in my car and go

One hundred and twenty up

The highway, windows rolled way down

Trying to feel anything

But this emptiness you left

It never quite eases the pain

But it's the closest thing I reach

That tastes like freedom from you

e.a.c.

"Because of You"

Foolish

He promised he would not leave me

Said he would always be by my side

Well here I am

And where is he

Life can be a real bitch, can't she

e.a.c.

Damaged Either Way

My parents always told me

Never get a tattoo

Never taint my perfect, God given body

Let me assure you

The buzzing of the needle moving at

Three thousand two hundred frames per second

Was soothing compared to

Screaming, calling me names

The sensation of the needle piercing my skin

Felt therapeutic compared to your hands on me

Every time you could not handle

Reality

This tattoo may last forever

But so will the scars you gave me

e.a.c.

"Because of You"

Bait

He said hello with a smile

Then left without a goodbye after a while

How dare he set this trap

Leave me in this enclosure

With absolutely no closure, full exposure

How could he reel me in like a fish

But leave me on the hook with no wish

Did he not see the sign

Catch and release only

Or did he plan to leave me lonely

I guess it's fine, I'll move on

In the dust I remain

Long gone

e.a.c.

"Because of You"

Toxic

Date me just to break me

Befriend me just to end me

Love me just to shove me

I am brittle and fragile

With a storm seething within me

You try to remake me

When it was you who broke me

I cannot be replicated by you

Don't expect to destroy me

And make beauty from my ruins

I am not yours to shape and mold

Fuck you for even trying

Only caring about my potential

Not that I am dying

e.a.c.

"Because of You"

Silent Killer

Physical Violence

Is blood and gore

Impossible to deny, to ignore

Mental violence

Is manipulative abuse

Yet is ignored, denied, let loose

Both just as brutal as the other

Yet one is acknowledged

One is invisible

Impossible to fight against

Impossible to find the criminal

e.a.c.

"Because of You"

Show Me Love

The only people who claim to love me

Are people who use me up

To them I am no companion

Rather a tool for their healing

I ease the pain, carry the burden

I scare away their demons

And when their demons dissipate, their burdens fly away,

Their pain subsides, my job done

I am completely abandoned

c.a.c.

"Because of You"

Goner

He never greeted her

Or said his goodbyes

Without it

They made her cheeks flush

Her heart race

It was the warmest embrace

Until

It

Turned

Cold

And she realized

It wasn't the kiss she missed

It was the boy behind it

e.a.c.

"Because of You"

Skin Deep

You're too skinny

She's too fat

Nice ass

Full rack

But no belly

If your arms and legs are like jelly

Then you're out of luck

Beauty is pain

Tears fall as she does one more

Push up

Lap

Sit up

But not too many

Or you might look masculine

God forbid, can't any of us girls win?

We all have beauty

Radiating within us

But if you can't get enough

Likes or Retweets

That kind of beauty

Does not count

e.a.c.

"Because of You"

Inequivalent

Have you ever feared

That people love you for your heart

Rather than your brain

Am I crazy that I don't

See these things the same

Or is it better

They only consider my heart

My mind is what makes me insane

I don't have any answers

I don't know if anyone else

Quite feels this way

Maybe we all do

I suppose we are all in dismay

e.a.c.

Truth

He tried to stretch it

She just told it

He manipulated it

I confided in it

He thought everyone was

Like him

I thought he was always

Like me

He hurt me with his lies

I cursed him with the truth

But now

I have been destroyed

And he is left wondering

Why he was

Such a monster

e.a.c.

"Because of You"

Eternal Winter

Baby it's cold outside

And it's not just the weather

Whenever we are not together

My feet get freezing

My fingers always numb

Maybe because you have me

Right under your thumb

Baby it's cold outside

Despite summer, winter, fall

When you're not with me at all

My cheeks start to hurt

My nose becomes all red

When you left me I should have fled

Left me with hypothermia, dead

Baby it's cold outside

You no longer give me your coat

You could have at least wrote a note

Here I lay remote

Baby it's cold outside

e.a.c.

"Because of You"

Telephone

Secrets, secrets

Are no fun

Unless you tell

Everyone

Until I know all about you

And the rest of the class does too

We'll all pass judgement

Never look at you the same

But trust us

Trust us

Let us embrace your shame

The class will whisper

Laugh and mock

Who knew your secret

Would leave blisters

Secrets, secrets

Are no fun

Unless you tell

Everyone

e.a.c.

"Because of You"

Insatiable

He had high hopes

And impressive

Expectations

Dedicated,

Motivated,

Driven,

His eyes set on

One thing only

More

He worked and pushed

Until one day

He reached his goal

And forgot how to

Live in the present

Always asking

What's next

Never enjoying

Right now

e.a.c.

Fortress

Whenever I see him

The inside of me melts

So my exterior grows hard

I want him to touch me

So I stand fifty feet away

I cannot deny my feelings

But I can put my walls up

I can pretend like seeing him

Doesn't give me butterflies that

Take flight deep in my chest

If you don't understand why I

Am hiding from him, building

Walls up higher than Everest

Then you have never been hurt like me

e.a.c.

"Because of You"

Drowning

When did the waves get so angry

Was it when man interrupted his still waters

Was it when the fulfilling life it held

      Could no longer live peacefully

Was it when the boats disrupted his slumber

Was it when man broke his calm little heart

      Because I know

When man interrupted my still waters

When I could no longer live peacefully

When I could never slumber

When man broke my little heart

      I was inconsolable

e.a.c.

Rebirth

When my parents got divorced

Nothing was mine anymore

Only Mom's or Dad's

When I was raped

My body was not mine anymore

It was stolen from me

When I love most more than they love me

I cannot even call myself theirs

I've got nothing left

But maybe these broken pieces of mine

Can create a new whole

That is almost just as good

e.a.c.

"Thanks to Me"

"Thanks to Me"

Sunshine

They called Van Gogh delirious

For swallowing yellow paint

To try and lift his spirits

But maybe he was onto something

Because as I sit here

Writing happier poems

No longer harming my precious body

My nails are painted like honey

My shirt like a bumblebee

And my spirits are indeed lifted

e.a.c.

"Thanks to Me"

Karma

Her memories

Haunt her,

Taunt her.

His memories

Please him,

Appease him.

But, oh

How the

Times have

Changed.

e.a.c.

Strength

I feel like I am drowning,

Until I remember I am the ocean.

I feel like I am suffocating,

Until I remember I am oxygen.

I feel like I am crashing and burning,

Until I remember I am a phoenix; rising from these ashes.

Do not let this world trick you

Into forgetting who you are:

A whole person, the sum of all of your parts.

e.a.c.

"Thanks to Me"

Why Do You Write So Often?

Maybe it is because this weight I carry

On my shoulders is too heavy,

But I know this paper's strength.

Or maybe because the constant motion of my steady hand

Puts my restless mind at ease.

e.a.c.

Why Do You Read So Often?

Well what kind of hypocrite would I be,

If I allowed other people to bear the weight of my paper

But I never helped them carry theirs?

e.a.c.

"Thanks to Me"

Necessary Summer Breeze

Windows rolled way down

Breeze flowing in my body

Like blood in my veins

e.a.c.

"Thanks to Me"

The Anthill

I look out the window to see crowds of students

Pouring in and out of buildings

Class has just ended and all of these

Students look identical from so far away

They all belong together

They are unidentifiable from my window

But when they look at each other

Passing by, all rushing away from the ringing bell

They only take note of each other's differences

Picking each other apart viciously

Leaving me to wish

That everyone had a window like mine

e.a.c.

"Thanks to Me"

Natural Beauty

Sometimes I feel as though I am the wind

She gives breaks in the sweltering heat,

She choreographs the trees dance effortlessly,

She carries seeds to their new home with care,

She gracefully leads sailboats on their journey,

She is a force to be reckoned with when let loose

Yet she is said to be unseen

And few and far between stop to appreciate

Her grace and splendor

e.a.c.

"Thanks to Me"

Stronger

My car slides off of the icy road

Right into a snow filled ditch

My heart should pound,

My hands freeze,

But the effects of this unforgiving weather

Have no effect on me anymore

e.a.c.

"Thanks to Me"

My Worst Fear

All she knew was change

She remained

Inconsistent, unpredictable

One day her hair was blonde,

The next blue

Tuesday she wore all black,

Wednesday she wore

Flowers in her hair

Unlike most,

She did not fear change

She was enraptured

By the wildness of it all

She only feared

Those who never learned

Their lessons,

Those who could not see

New perspectives,

What she feared most

Was the unchanged heart

e.a.c.

Children

Innocent and pure

Be careful, be gentle

They are always

Laughing, crying

Hugging, playing

As I grow into adulthood

I wish that we

Were not so afraid

To simply *feel*

e.a.c.

Polar Opposite

I used to be white

Blank like an empty page

Just waiting to be filled up

But now I am black

Like the words on this page

That push me through the emptiness

e.a.c.

Ode to a Stoner

Go back to therapy,

Is what they told me.

So I went to my car,

Cruise around not too far,

Grind up my plant,

Light it up, watch it burn

This is my therapy.

It is not a doctor telling me what I already know,

It is a relief.

Getting high when I'm feeling low,

Just by myself I don't make it a show.

I blow out the smoke,

It sets me free,

Is this what it's like to be happy?

Not quite, but I am close.

They call it getting high,

But it keeps me grounded.

e.a.c.

"Thanks to Me"

Where the Heart Is

There's something about the

Constellations out in space,

The way they glimmer and sparkle,

Just for me.

There's something about the moon,

Waxing, waning,

The way it opens its arms to me.

There's something about the

Night sky,

Calling me, reassuring me,

Come on home.

e.a.c.

Confidence

Her teeth were crooked,

> And a little yellow.

Her eyes were different sizes,

> And sort of lopsided.

Her nose was gigantic,

> And very uneven.

Her feet were long,

> And pretty clumsy.

She was too curvy,

> And a little lofty.

Her stretch marks showed,

> Along with some cellulite.

Everything about her was imperfect,

Ugly even.

But she doused herself in love,

And her reflection began

To look a little better.

e.a.c.

Nature's Remedy

Easily clearing

Out my dusty, cobwebbed mind

With God's gift: fresh air

e.a.c.

Moving Day

The wheels spun

Within her mind

Creativity,

Imagination,

The only things

She refused

To leave behind

e.a.c.

"Thanks to Me"

Paradox

I am a conundrum

I feel free in my cage

I only stop when I feel I'll continue on forever

I am empty, and overflowing

I do not care, but everything matters to me

I am connected to the universe, but feel so small

I relate to everyone, yet remain alone

I am confusing, and head spinning

But I am content

e.a.c.

Embrace your experience

This life you live

Is quite deceiving

It seems you have forever,

But only when you look back

Do you realize your moments

Were fleeting.

So soak in

This regular, humdrum day,

Tomorrow everything may

Change

e.a.c.

Trust the Journey

Instead of throwing my hands

Up in the air

And asking,

Why God, why?

I will keep

My head held high

And ask,

Why not?

e.a.c.

"Thanks to Me"

What is happiness anyways?

I struggle to write

Joyous poems

And I thought it was

Because of the circumstances

Always living in tender, delightful misery

But I have since realized

It is actually because

The things that make me happiest

Are just harder to describe

In a way that does them justice

e.a.c.

"Thanks to Me"

How to Have the Happiest Life

I am always so full

Not because of what I have

But because of everything I give

e.a.c.

Daydreamer

My goldfish

Swims around his bowl,

Never tired of his

Repetitive pattern.

How happy I am,

That I refuse to live

Like my goldfish

e.a.c.

"Thanks to Me"

Live for the Excitement

Time is an imaginary concept

Made by man

That we are not

Guaranteed

Yet we plan our lives

According to

Days,

Months, and

Years

That we may not be given

Keep hoping for more,

But please

Enjoy this moment

It's all you will have for sure

e.a.c.

Renewed

Time is flying by

And I used to stroll,

But now I sprint

The difference in pace

Is quite enthralling

e.a.c.

"Thanks to Me"

Chapter One

For each death a new life,

For each tear endless laughter,

For every failure a success,

For every bad day there is some good

Each and every desolate ending

Brings a bright new beginning

Fear no more, dear child

e.a.c.

"Thanks to Me"

Connected

Have you ever thought that

Although many people have

A fleeting existence in your life,

They go home to children, and

Loved ones, and experience hardship

While you go home and endure the same?

So open the door for them,

Pay for their check,

Say please and thank you,

Do what you can,

Because when a stranger does that for you

They have more than a fleeting existence

In your day, week, year,

Your life

e.a.c.

"Thanks to Me"

Home

The mountains so green

People and weather so warm

Fresh air so wholesome

e.a.c.

I am Fictional

When I flip the pages,

I feel excitement

Like these words can

Empathize with me

Like these characters

Understand every

Fiber of my being

When I read, I do not read to understand

I read so someone understands me

e.a.c.

"Thanks to Me"

Man's Best Friend

A small dog

Licked away her

Salty tears

He could not resolve

All of life's problems

But he

Sure did help

e.a.c.

Leap of Faith

I took a chance

To change my fate

I took a leap

And filled with regret

I saw how short I was going to fall

Falling,

      Falling,

            Falling

Until I opened my eyes

Finding myself

In a better place

All because

A shot in the dark

Led me to the light

e.a.c.

Life Raft

I used to think

Others were the problem

Watching me sink

And never helping me onto their boat

But here I am

No longer drowning

Because I taught myself to swim

And I will be the difference

Trying to teach others like me

That they, too, can liberate themselves

e.a.c.

Faith in Humanity

Put your faith in others

Not faith that they will not fail you

But faith that you will forgive,

They will grow,

And you both will prosper

e.a.c.

"Thanks to Me"

Power of Positivity

We tend to dwell on

Bad luck

Catching up to us

These unlucky circumstances

Are out of our control,

We try to place blame

But if we just keep

Trudging onward

Good luck will find us

More often

e.a.c.

"Thanks to Me"

Gracious

The world owes us nothing

The universe has granted us life

Never will I look at another brother

And say he has more than I

Always I will humble myself

Grateful for struggles,

Grateful for losses,

Grateful for others' presence

Humble yourself

None of us belong here

Yet this beautiful gift of life

Was bestowed upon us

e.a.c.

You Deserve to be the Sun

The moon held such an

Adoration

For the sun

That he periodically

Gave himself away

To be with her

To humans, this is known as

The phases of the moon

e.a.c.

"Thanks to Me"

I, the Rock, You, the River

A strong, rushing current

Sweeping away

Everything in its path

Or so it thought

Until the river met the rock

The current went

Over,

Under,

Around,

But could not push through

Funny how a thing so pure

Can be stopped by

Something so sure

e.a.c.

Breaking Bad Habits

Smoke gently flows from my mouth

Pouring into my car as

Music gently plays from my radio

It's funny how this reminds me of days

When you'd pack me a bowl

Maybe roll us a blunt

Windows down, jams turned up

Marijuana always making me smile

You made me laugh every once in a while

I gave you up, but I kept the weed

Now I'm alone, but I have what I need

e.a.c.

Late for a Reason

I was late for my train

Had to wait for the next time

But he was perfectly on schedule

And I caught his eye, like he did mine

He sat next to me

The whole ride

I wouldn't say it was

Good karma

I would call it

Serendipity

Because now

We take the train together

Every morning

And go to our home together

Every night

e.a.c.

"Thanks to Me"

Riley Joseph

Everyone has a smile

Each as beautiful and unique

As the other

But one lucky girl

Had a brother with a smile

That made her

Beam with delight

A smile that was different

In the best possible

Way

And she got to keep it

All to herself

Because her smile

Was different

In the best possible

Way

To him, too

e.a.c.

"Thanks to Me"

Together we Light up a Room

I had felt heat before

From things such as the sun's rays

But before this

Never has my

Heart,

Body,

Mind,

Soul

Exuded such warmth

Produced simply by our laughter

e.a.c.

"Thanks to Me"

Seth Owen

They held a nonverbal pact

An unspoken promise

Whether they grew together

Or apart

They would eternally protect

One another

It was something

Unexplainable and beautiful

Neither had to call

They were always just

There

e.a.c.

Safe Place

When I am in this house,

The world outside stops.

Everything troublesome ceases to exist,

It's just us.

All so connected that-

You can barely tell where

One of us ends, and another begins.

Everything here is euphoric,

I know when I step outside reality

Will creep back in,

But we don't have to worry about that yet.

Not here.

e.a.c.

"Thanks to Me"

In my Father's Arms

Protected,

Safe,

Constantly guiding me,

Saving me from myself,

And this desolate world around me

e.a.c.

My Very Own Sistine Chapel

His eyebrows furrowed and thick

His eyelashes delicate, long

His hair shaggy and unkept

His button nose

His deep, never-ending eyes

His soft lips, freshly kissed

His sloppy grin, dimples and all

His lean and muscular arms

His goofy personality

His hazel eyes, russet hair,

Ebony features

His calming voice

His booming laugh

The way he looks at me

He's such a work of art

e.a.c.

"Thanks to Me"

Role Models

My brother says I'm not funny,

But as he tells my same joke

To his friends the next day,

I know he thinks I am hilarious.

My brother says he hates me,

But as he goes to school and writes

A paper about me, his hero,

I know that he loves me.

My brother says that I'm stupid,

But as he asks me for advice

And needs help on his homework,

I know he thinks I am the smartest girl in the world.

e.a.c.

"Thanks to Me"

For my Mama

My mother is

Like a wolf

She has the instinct

To bare her sharp teeth

But she can always

Soften her grip

When she has to hold me

e.a.c.

"Thanks to Me"

New beginnings

We sat on the porch swing

Listening to the birds sing

Speaking of substance our life did bring

Prosperity, torment, everything

What a perfect first day of spring

These are the days worth worshipping

e.a.c.

Survivor

He cowers quickly

Not as a sign of weakness

But as a sign of vigor

e.a.c.

"Thanks to Me"

Church

Heaven or

Reincarnation

It's all the same to me

Jesus, Buddha

Guru, Ala

Muhammad, God

It's all the same to me

But as I walk into

This building on Sundays

And feel the chatter

Radiating between

Brothers and Sisters

I know I can put all my faith

In this love

e.a.c.

"Thanks to Me"

Mutual

His branches grew

So far and wide

His fruit he bared

Was ripe and nectarous

He gave it all to her

And she gave him the world

They were a perfect pair

He gave shelter, she gave care

Together they grew until

Their souls intertwined

Together forever

Until the end of time

e.a.c.

The Love I Deserve

He looks at me like he is starving

And I am the only thing on this

Goddamn planet

That could fully satisfy him

And I look at him

Like I am parched

And as if he is the only thing in the

Goddamn desert

That could fully satiate me

e.a.c.

"Thanks to Me"

Watching a Sad Movie with my Best Friend

My very favorite thing to do

Because you are distraught and isolated

Until you look beside you

And they are feeling the same things

So you cannot be as troubled or lonesome

It's the perfect balance

Recognizing that we all feel like shit

But we are feeling it together

And maybe that's what makes it all worth it

e.a.c.

"Thanks to Me"

Memories Calling Me

Raspy, Deep, Bold, and Course

Gruff, but gentle when speaking to

His precious granddaughter

The whispers and secrets they shared

Felt like home

Oh what that little girl

Wouldn't give

To hear that sweet voice

Once more

e.a.c.

"Thanks to Me"

Bliss

Running around the yard

Barefoot and certainly sweaty

Laughing so hard that

Apple juice squirts from your nose

And then laughing even harder

My childhood was never perfect

But I swear to God

Those summer days always were

e.a.c.

"Thanks to Me"

Soulmates

No matter how close

We get to someone

There will always be

Cells between us and the person we want

To touch the most

Meaning we never

Really touch anyone

But you and I are different

When we embrace

I feel it in my bones

Our love is so strong

Cells and bacteria scatter

Just so we can touch

e.a.c.

These are the Days

Every Sunday

Cars fill the driveway

And the children play outside

The men are out in the barn

Us girls on the porch

Everyone eating dinner together

Every Sunday

Always laughing

Memories we'll cherish

Quality time well spent

Taking these days for granted, maybe

But never ignoring the love

Every Sunday

e.a.c.

Beauty and Grace

She is rickety

Losing her sight and vision

But still just as strong

e.a.c.

"Thanks to Me"

Synchronized

Even though he cannot speak

He says a lot to me

And as we lay together

Talking about how our day went

In silence

My heart fills with a joy

That no one else quite

Understands

e.a.c.

"Thanks to Me"

Thank You

Not to say

I did it all on my own

Or that

Everything is perfect now

But I am

Constantly getting better

Even when I

Regress and am depressed

I know

That I can bounce back

And my

Mindset is much healthier

Despite anyone else

Thanks to me

And those offering

Their unwavering support

Throughout my journey

e.a.c.

Made in the USA
Lexington, KY
23 March 2018